AN INDISPENSABLE GUIDE

BET ON YOUR GOLF GAME!

FOR BETTING ON THE GOLF COURSE

RALPH MONTI

Published by GolfBooks
Upper Montclair, New Jersey

Published by:
GolfBooks, a division of: Fortune Media Inc.
P.O. Box 43238
Upper Montclair
New Jersey 07043

Copyright © 1994 by Ralph Monti
Printed in the United States of America

Monti, Ralph.
    Bet on your golf game! : an indispensible guide for betting on the golf course / Ralph Monti.
    p. cm.
    Preassigned LCCN: 93-074488
    ISBN 1-884490-20-4

    1. Golf—Betting.   I. Title

GV979.B47M65 1994   796.352
                                QBI93-22461

For group, premium or bulk purchases, contact GolfBooks for discount schedule.

Illustrations by Jon Wardell

To Margaret,
for all the fun we have playing golf.

Acknowledgment

There are several people who I'd like to thank and acknowledge for the inspiration of this book.

First off, thanks to Steve Zammarchi, my indefatigable golf partner, who, week in and out, treks out to the wilds of the suburbs where he joins me in (what seems like) our futile quest for golfing excellence.

Thanks also to Jack Stuart and Bill Steele. Jack and Bill's ongoing betting games throughout our weekly rounds were, unbeknownst to them, the initial spark for this book.

And finally, thanks to Steve Holly, the production brains behind the book. Steve worked weekends and late evenings to meet every deadline that was thrown at him. He's done a terrific job designing an easy-to-read guide for golfers everywhere.

Table of Contents

So Waddya Wanna Bet?

If you're like me, there's probably no other place you'd rather spend a weekend or a day away from work than on a golf course. Why is that? Why are we so caught up with this game? Why do we spend countless hours playing, reading, practicing, talking about, watching, lamenting and (hopefully) bragging about our game? What is it about this game that gets us so crazy? Marriages are ruined. Romances are destroyed. Jobs are lost. All because of golf. My explanation of why we get so addicted is one that stems from our childhood. From our days in school.

Consider this: Golf is the only sport we play where each of us must carry a report card in our back pocket. Unlike tennis or other individual sports, golf makes us record our ongoing, up-to-the-minute performance. The psychic tangibility of that silly card is one of the game's great motivators. Think about it. Like the report card from our younger days, our golf report card chronicles our day: our good "grades" are recorded as eagles, birdies and pars; our failing grades are entered as bogeys, double-bogeys and, well, you get the point. Similarly, most of us celebrate our good scores in the same way our good grades were treated in grammar school. A school report card adorned with little gold stars shows a star student. A golf card with lots of circled or starred scores on it shows a golfer of exceptional ability. A card with no stars indicates a bad or, at best, a mediocre player. A card with lots of circles at the end of the day gives cause for celebration. And, let's face it, how many of us, never satisfied with just bragging about a great round, stuff the card in our pocket to show it off to the folks back home? Golf is the ultimate individual sport, where your only opponents are a little white ball and that damn report card in your pocket.

So what does this have to do with betting on your golf game? Lots. We all know money is a great motivator. When someone bets you to "put your money where your mouth is," they're challenging you to show them your best golf game. To have a great round. To get lots of circles on your golf report card. So winning a golf bet becomes the ultimate gold star. And the funny thing is, the struggle for that ultimate gold star becomes that much sweeter. You can win a few dollars or several thousand dollars, but the real excitement flows from the contest. The pitched battle that gets your juices flowing to win the best gold star. The level you take yourself to focus into your game. The magical rhythm you get into as you float through the course. And the interesting thing is, these feelings are shared by many golfers around the country. Magazine polls show that golfers enjoy a round more when they have money on the line. These are golfers playing on country club or public courses. And even more interesting is that the size of the bet isn't that important. How true. I've played just as hard for a 25¢ bet as I have for a $25 bet. And the golf shots I remember best are the ones I made to win a bet. And I'm sure so have you.

Bet on Your Golf Game! will show you some terrific bets to add spice to your golf. It will show you how to put more fun into an already exciting game. For the sake of economy, I've chosen bets where you can easily factor in handicap strokes. The bets range from the elementary to the more complex. Start off with the easy games first, and don't bet over your head.

Enjoy the book !

-Ralph Monti

Stroke
and
Match
Play

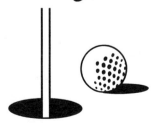

Stroke and match play are the basic betting games in golf. In fact, most of the bets that are described in the following pages have their roots in these contests.

Let's look at stroke play first. Stroke play is what the professional tournaments use to decide who's going to win The Masters or the U.S. Open. It's the tournament format played on television. The winner of the round is the player who finishes 18 holes with the fewest amount of strokes. A stroke is defined as an attempt to hit the ball. Stroke play takes patience, diligence and the ability to focus on your game through the highs and lows of a round. It's a lot like life. You can have a double bogey run and be a bum one minute, and then get hot and roll out a couple of birdies the next.

Either way, you don't face the music until the end of the day. And, the music can either be sweet like a Beatles melody, or somber like a Wagner funeral dirge. Either way your fate is judged at the end.

Match play, on the other hand, offers either instant gratification or disappointment. There's no waiting for the round to end to see how you're going to fare. This reason alone makes match play the more popular form of betting among amateur golfers. Match play is betting your game hole to hole, and you play to beat your opponent on one particular hole. Once the hole is ended and a winner is declared, you move on to the next hole where the slate is cleaned and a new bet starts. So, essentially, you have eighteen little contests during a round. Match play gets very interesting when you begin assigning additional monetary values to certain holes. Par 5s or low handicap holes can be worth more to the winner than a par 4, for instance. We'll get into these other bets later on. There are derivative games spun from match play, too. One such game is match vs. par, where par is your opponent. If you score lower than a par, you take a +1, and a -1 if you score over par. You get a zero if you par. The player who is most up on par after the round, wins.

Keep in mind, of course, that the same rules apply whether you're playing head to head against one opponent, or you're playing team play. In match play among teams, you use the best score between partners to determine who wins the hole. If it's a draw, you can either throw out the hole or carry the hole over to play a skin.

Playing
Skins

Chances are you probably won't recognize the name Don Ohlmeyer. Don is a television producer who made a name for himself as the executive producer of NBC Sports. Although he did an outstanding job producing sports for the Peacock network, his real claim to fame is being known as the marketing genius who came up with the widely popular Skins Game, a golf phenomenon on network televison that he started in 1983. Skins is a game that's been around for a long, long time, but Ohlmeyer had the genius to envision it as a game that the pros could play for high drama (and big bucks). More about him in a minute.

Skins is match play, only with a twist. Each hole is given a point or monetary value. The only thing you and your opponents need to figure out before you start a round is the amount of monetary value you want to assign each hole. Usually, the harder holes are assigned the highest monetary value, the easiest holes the least amount of money, and so on. The player with the lowest score on the hole wins the hole and is awarded the "skin." In the event of a tie, the predetermined value of the hole is carried over to the next hole, making the carryover that much more valuable. Chances are you and I will play skins for money that isn't considered "high drama." Enter Don Ohlmeyer.

Ohlmeyer was smart enough to recognize a simple game that could be turned into a great television contest that would burst the Saturday and Sunday afternoon ratings balloon. He invites four marquee pros to play a skins game on national television in which each hole is assigned a monetary value of stratospheric proportions. In the event a hole is tied, a carryover would apply, meaning that Jack, Arnie, Tom and Lee could presumably be playing for a hole worth as much as the gross national product of some countries. Needless to say, the annual tournament instantly became a hit with viewers around the country drooling in their La-Z-Boys, making skins one of the most popular games on the country's golf courses.

Skin
Slalom

If you had to pick one sport that you thought was similar to golf, what sport would it be? During a sports seminar I attended several years ago I was asked this question. The sport I chose was downhill skiing. In my mind, downhill skiing and golf share the same mental skills. Both sports pit the individual against nature. To be a successful golfer or skier you must have a keen sense for terrain, wind, and weather. In skiing, it's you against the mountain. In golf, it's you against the course. Both sports have hazards that come into play. Sand traps and ski moguls are as great a mental challenge as they are physical ones. Both demand intense concentration and mental resiliency. Lose your concentration on the mountain, and you'll probably fall on your butt. Let your mind drift on the course and watch those double bogeys add up. In a race, the better skier has the ability to focus in on improving his time after he hits a few bumpy stretches down the mountain. The more experienced golfer knows how to put a triple bogey hole behind him and not let it ruin his round. In competitive downhill racing, you're only as good as your last gate. In golf, you're only as good as the last hole. So, the next time you're on the course, think of the holes as a series of ski gates. But make sure you pack the cleats instead of the boots.

Skin Slalom has nothing to do with skiing, but it does start with each player throwing a certain amount of money into a pot. Under match play rules, the golfer with the lowest score wins a skin. If a player wins the hole with a natural birdie, the hole is worth two skins. Tied holes are not carried over. Once the round is finished, you divide the number of skins won into the total value of the pot. Here's an example: four players throw in $25 apiece in the pot. The total pot is $100. If 10 skins are won during the round, each skin is worth $10. You then divvy up the skins to the appropriate winner(s).

Because of the way it "evens out" the holes, Skin Slalom has both advantages and disadvantages, depending on what type of golfer you are. If you're an accurate long ball hitter who scores well on long yardage par 5s, you might want to play regular skins where the par 5s usually (but not always) have a greater monetary value. In this way, you're playing into your strength. On the other hand, if your game lends itself more to consistency than long ball, then Skin Slalom is the game for you.

Bets to
Carry in
Your Bag

Bingo, Bango, Bongo

   Bingo, Bango, Bongo is one of the basic betting games in golf. Played hole to hole, a player collects points as follows:

   First on the green ....1 point
   Closest to the pin ....1 point
   First to hole out.............1 point

   Add some extra fun to the game by doubling the bet if one player sweeps all points on the hole, or tripling the bet if a player sweeps the points with a birdie.

Poleys

   I've played two variations of this game. The first one is where a player earns a poley point if he drains a putt longer than the length of the flag stick. A dollar value is declared for a poley point before the round.

At the end of the round the poley points are added up and the bets are disbursed accordingly.

The second variation is where a player gains a point by hitting his tee shot on a par 3 green within stick distance of the cup. This game can be scored two ways. If a second player hits a tee shot inside another player's tee shot, the ball lying farthest away is nullified. Or both can earn a point so long as they are within flag stick distance of the cup. Decide before you start your round.

Greenies

Greenies are tee shots on par 3s that land closest to the pin. Some golfers play that you must get the par to collect a greenie, while others pay the greenie outright. Greenies on individual holes can double in value if you birdie the hole. Side bets include paying double to an individual player or team who sweeps all par 3 greenies. If no one wins a greenie on a par 3, then the greenie bet is doubled on the next par 3. If a player birdies that par 3, he's paid four times the first bet.

Sandies

Sandies is a bet where a player hits into a greenside bunker and still makes par on the hole. Sandies have a fixed point or dollar value during a round. A Super Sandie is when a player hits into a fairway and greenside bunker, and still makes par. Super Sandies pay double.

Whiskey
Down

Most New York City folks like to have tuna fish on "whiskey down," a term busy waiters shout at short order cooks when ordering toasted rye bread. Several years ago, my friend Al and I were sitting in a greasy spoon munching away on a couple of tuna fish on whiskey down sandwiches. Al is one of those gamblers who's always looking for a little action. He just can't sit still without making a bet. Suddenly, like he was goosed by a 200-volt cattle prod, Al jumps up from his seat and with his big, meaty hand swoops up a slice of rye bread from his sandwich. He challenges me to a bet. How many caraway seeds are embedded in the slice. Which side? I ask sarcastically. Both sides plus the crust, he challenges. I couldn't believe he could think of betting on something like this. But almost as fast as you can say tuna melt, he's got the whole diner playing our game, with an old guy sporting a bad toupee acting as the caraway seed counter. The game went on for almost two hours. Who says you can't find any action in a New York diner?

When you play Whiskey Down on the golf course, you aren't counting caraway seeds, you're counting points. Before you start playing Whiskey Down, you and your opponent must establish a dollar value on points that you might win. Each hole has a five-point potential: low score on the hole gets you two points, two points are awarded for a natural birdie and one point for closest to the pin. If a player wins all five points, the bet is usually doubled or tripled. So, if you establish a point at, let's say, $5 per, you've got yourself some very good action. You can also mix and match other plays for points, too. You could award one point for a sandie, for instance, to make the game more interesting.

If you're giving strokes to a higher handicap player, you can also play for low net, depending on how generous you are or how badly he plays. The great thing about Whiskey Down is that there are so many ways to bet a hole. Your imagination is your limit. Think of my friend Al next time you need inspiration.

Golf
Rotisserie

"DRAIN IT GREG!" "CHIP IT IN PAUL!"

Three days into my honeymoon, my bride and I were out shooting a round on one of Long Island's best courses. It was a day for the books because I was having one of those rounds that you dream of. Every shot was dropping down on the green as softly as a windblown feather. Birdie, par, birdie, par, I went. Suddenly around the 14th, a lumbar disc kicks out, but I stubbornly played on. There's no way I was going to give up this round! By the time I get to the 18th green, I'm swinging my clubs like a slumped-over gorilla searching for a lost banana. As I crawled into the clubhouse with pretzel-like rigor mortis, I realize I've done myself in. Not only for the rest of the honeymoon (which was fodder for a lot of jokes), but for the rest of the summer, too. The closest I get to golf that year was bird dogging the pros and betting on their game.

Even if you're sitting up straight these days, you can have lots of fun betting on golf pros. For want of a better name I call this game Golf Rotisserie. In case you've been living in a cave in Outer Mongolia, rotisserie is a term more synonymous with baseball. Rotisserie Baseball is a game in which fans make up teams from a pool of professional players. Most of the time there's a pot, and you win or lose money depending on the performance of your players. Golf Rotisserie operates the same way.

Before the professional golf season starts, get together with a bunch of friends and draw cards or pick numbers out of a hat, which correspond to golfers on the pro tour. You may want to draw from a player field limited to the top ten professional players. And just in case your pro goes down with a season-ending back injury, you'll want to pick alternates. From there set up a pot in which everybody contributes an equal amount. Then be creative and structure a point system based on tournaments won, majors won, biggest earnings made, etc. You can also set up a negative point system based on variables like missing a tournament cut, not finishing in the top five or anything else that comes into you mind. To have two golf rotisseries going at once, set up another game tracking the senior players. It's a great way to keep your interest piqued on the pro tours.

Call It
and
Pick Nine

On January 9, 1969, Joe Namath sat in a poolside chaise in Miami and made the boast of the decade. He guaranteed winning Super Bowl III against the 18-point favorite Baltimore Colts. His "I think we'll win it; in fact, I'll guarantee it" quip hit the sports pages like a ton of bricks. The New York Jets were an upstart team from an upstart league challenging the invincibility of the National Football League. They were a bunch of long-haired, cocky players led by a quarterback who loved to thumb his nose at the establishment. Stodgy NFL types were in shock. Who was this braggadocio? We're going to teach him a lesson, several of the Colts said. But Namath and the Jets backed up those words. They went on to stun the Colts with a 16-7 victory.

There are several bets in golf where you can predict and play like Joe Namath, and although you might not become a national hero and go on to become a multi-millionaire celebrity, you'll get great pleasure backing up your boasts with actions. Call It is one such game. All you have to do is predict your final round score. The player who comes the closest without going over the score wins. Any amount of wager can be made on this game, of course, and it's a great side bet when other action is in play. To make things interesting, call your front and back round scores, too. This way, you'll have a couple of shots at cleaning up the pot.

A variation of Call It is the bet Pick Nine. Before you head out on the course, each player must declare nine holes throughout the round that he wishes to put "in play." The nine holes that you declare are your action holes, meaning those are the holes you're calling and betting on. The player who racks up the most holes wins the pot.

Take the Snake, Barkies, and Woodrows

"FIVE TO ONE HE OVERSHOOTS
THE GREEN."

Ever have one of those days when natural wildlife scares the living daylights out of you? Happened to me one early summer morning while I was playing a round on a marshy, back country course in Florida. Florida is a state where golfing can be a wildlife expedition, with gators bellying up greenside to gaze at fools sporting funny hats and Ozzie Nelson slacks. While gators don't particularly send chills down my spine (although you'd have to come up with a lot of coin for me to wrestle one), the one varmint that does give me the willies is the snake. I was about mid-swing off the backside of the green near a water hazard on the first hole, when this big ol' snake slithers right on by. He was sporting a dancing tongue and all. Needless to say, I watched my back on every hole I played after that, feeling like a wanted mobster eating in a busy downtown restaurant.

Snake or Take the Snake is a game that penalizes 3-putt putting. During the round, the first player to 3-putt a green carries the snake and holds onto the snake until another player 3-putts and takes the snake. The player that holds the snake after nine and eighteen then pays out to all the other players a set amount of money agreed upon beforehand. This bet will force you to concentrate on stroking through the ball!

A barkie (or woodrow) is a game that, simply put, rewards you for making something good out of something bad. This bet takes into account your play around trees rather than wildlife. A barkie or woodrow describes a player who's made par after he's hit a tree trunk, limb, or branch. Usually, a betting group will have one or two barkies going into play, with a set amount of money set aside for each.

Bogey

There are certain times when you know you're out of your league. Like the time I was working in a gun and ammo shop throwing the bull around, claiming to be the best shot in the neighborhood. Funny stuff when you consider the closest I've ever been to a gun was a .45 plastic water pistol. But somehow if you sell guns and ammo to weekend hunters and you've got a terrific gift for bull, you can have most people believe you're an expert. So there I am holding court telling a big game hunter about my latest hunting expedition. Except this guy decides to call my bluff. He starts challenging me to ride down to his ranch and shoot with him. And how he wants to invite his big game brother-in-law to hunt with me, too. It took several weeks to backpedal my way out of that one, instantly curing an insatiable habit for throwing the bull.

Bogey is a no-bull game for low handicap players. This game will cost you big time if you don't have what it takes. Some of the pros you see on TV honed their skills and fattened their wallets playing Bogey. Pure and simple, the object of the game is to shoot par or better golf. Pure and simple, don't score a bogey. As I said, this game is for big hitters with heavy wallets. A set amount of money is decided upon per hole. Usually lots. If one player bogeys, he pays those that didn't bogey the hole the agreed-upon sum. He continues to pay the agreed-upon sum on subsequent holes until another player bogeys. Then that golfer starts paying out. It continues that way until yet another golfer bogeys, who then assumes the payout. The way to make big bucks, of course, is not to bogey a hole. This way, you'll get paid 18 times whatever the holes are worth. Once the round is over, you compute your payouts.

For those golfers with less nerve and higher handicaps, you can play a variation of the game using double bogey as the benchmark. All the rules of Bogey apply.

Bong

Sister Olivia was my first grade teacher, and she really got a kick out of intimidating little children. An imposing nun who stood close to six feet tall, her life's passion was to torment frisky six-year-old students who had the audacity to misbehave in her class. Her favorite pastime was having a naughty pupil crawl under her desk, and at certain periods during the course of one's imprisonment, subject them to her sudden, swift kicks. Depending on your offense, you could be under her desk for hours, all at the whimsy of Sister's Olivia's mood. The class called her imprisonment "bong"- as in "Vinnie got bonged by Sister Olivia today." It's funny that such a term exists in golf and that it's keyed to one's transgressions on the golf course. Maybe

Sister Olivia was a passionate golfer?

Bong is a game that assesses points to a player when he's playing bad. The player who collects the largest number of bong points through the round must pay the other players. Bong points are set up as follows:

Complete whiff	4 points
Lost ball	2
Out-of-bounds ball	2
Sand trap	1
Water hazard	1
Two out of the sand trap	3
Three out of the sand	4
Three putt	3
Four putt	4

The point here is not to win this game. You want to play as well as you can, otherwise you'll be getting kicked under the desk by Sister Olivia.

Nassau
and
Press Bets

Nassau and press bets are two fundamental bets in golf that you will enjoy once you start betting on your golf game. They are probably the most frequently played bets and probably the most fun. While press bets may seem complicated at first, they do make for a very entertaining wrinkle during a round of golf.

Nassau is a series of bets that's set up three ways. You bet on your play on the first nine holes, the second nine holes and the overall round. Winning a nassau is based on match play. So if you win more holes against your opponent on the front nine, you'll take a nassau. Win more holes on the back nine, and you gain a second nassau. Take more holes than your opponent on the overall 18, you've won yet another nassau. Tied holes can be pushed to the next hole or thrown out. Nassaus can be bet for any amount of money.

Press bets are interesting wrinkles when playing nassaus, and are new bets, declared usually when a player is two holes down to his opponent. They are declared because the losing player wants to initiate a new bet with the hopes of nullifying his losing play or drawing even. When a player presses, the original bet is still in play, so any win or loss on subsequent holes from the press bet is applied to the original bet. At the hole the player presses, a new bet is begun, and play is carried forward. You then keep score of two bets, the original and the press bet. If the player who was originally winning begins to lose, and happens to go two down, then he can declare a press bet. Now you'll have three bets going.

Here's an example. If I'm playing Steve and he's two up on me after two holes, I will press to start a new bet. Now let's say I win the next four holes. Not only have I drawn even on the original bet, I'm now two up on the press bet. Because he's two down, Steve presses my press bet. Let's say that when the smoke clears after nine, I've won the original bet by +1, and my press bet by +2. Steve won his press bet +1. I win the nassau because I've won one more bet. When computing press bets, only the number of bets won count, not the total number of holes.

One Half Combined Vs. One

Do you know what's even better than beating one opponent? Beating two. Whether its golf, racquetball, tennis, billiards or table tennis, I've always relished the challenge of taking on two players at once. If you win and you're playing with odds, chances are you can win a nice tidy sum. There are several games in golf where you can play against two players. An example is One Half Combined Vs. One, a game that gets everybody into the action.

Playing with three players, one player is selected to play against the other two for the first six holes. To win the hole, the lone player must shoot a score better than 1/2 the combined score of the other two. Here's an example. Let's say I'm playing against Steve and Ed on the first hole. I shoot a par 4. Steve takes a 6 and Ed shoots a bogey 5. Their combined score (5 + 6 =11 ÷ 2= 5-1/2) is 5-1/2 . Since I've shot a 4, I win the hole. After my six holes of playing against the other two, Steve now becomes the lone player. At the 13th hole, Ed is the lone player against me and Steve. The betting can be determined in a variety of ways. Each hole can have a value, plus each round of six can have a set pot, too. Whatever way you set it up, One Half Combined vs. One is a great threesome game, especially when your fourth player has decided to sleep in.

Yardage
and
Double Up

You know that funny little character who's on those yellow Community Chest Monopoly cards? One card shows him with a sad look on his face as he stands holding his pockets inside out. That's because he's lost all his money and he's heading for the poorhouse. Yardage and Double Up are games that could send you to the poorhouse, too. If you lose these games, you'll end up standing in the 19th hole with nothing left in your pockets.

Yardage is a golf bet that's scored by the yard. In other words, your winnings are determined by the hole yardage you've won. So, for instance, if you've won 12 holes that total 3600 yards and you're playing 10¢ per hole, you're up $360. But before you collect your winnings, you have to figure out your opponent's yardage winnings. The difference is awarded to the final winner. It doesn't take a genius to see that this game gets real expensive and usually favors the accurate long ball hitters who score well on long par 5s. The key word is "accurate," of course.

For those golfers with champagne tastes, high-rent living, and non-yip putting, try Double Up. When this bet is on, each hole, starting with the first, doubles cumulatively in value. And you get to carry over tie holes. So let's say you start on the first hole playing for 10¢. The 8th hole would then be worth $12.80, at the 15th you'd be playing for $1,638.40 and by the 18th the pot reaches $13,067.20. And these are pot values without any carryovers! This game obviously isn't for everyone, but you could adjust the game to fit your wallet. If you don't, you could find yourself bankrupt without passing Go.

Round
Robin

When was the last time any of you good ol' boys went square dancing? Wrangled into some blue jeans and slipped on some snakeskins to dance the dos-à-dos with Elly May or Miss Kitty? The kick outta dancing square, partner, is the amount of fair-haired ladies you get to dance with, what with all them dos-à-dos, haymaker's jigs, Texas stars, and little brown jug dances. So if you like a lotta partners, partner, then Round Robin is for you.

Round Robin is a game that claims its origin from the courses of the Lone Star State. In their big friendly way, Texans get a kick out of meeting new folk and this game will certainly do that for you. The game is played as a foursome and everybody changes partners every six holes. By the time you finish your round, you'd have part-nered with everybody in the group. While playing as partners, all kinds of bets can be played: low ball, low total, team shooting a birdie, etc. The fun is playing with the differ-ent player, especially if you're in a newly mixed group.

Blind Round Robin offers yet another wrinkle to the game. In this game, you go out and play your round with your group. After finishing play, everybody's name is thrown into a hat (use a ten-gallon or Stetson in honor of the game's origins) and then draw partners for succeeding holes. From there compute who's done what and with whom to deter-mine the winners. Stroke play is the best sys-tem to determine a winner and/or the win-ning team when playing a Round Robin game.

Bag a
Squirrel
and
Hawk

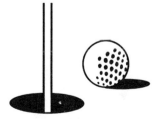

My dog Heidi is a German Shorthaired Pointer who has the energy of a dynamo. She's also one of the smartest canines I've had the pleasure to walk. When I bought her some years ago, I told the breeder I wanted a pointer that wasn't too hyper. Yeah, right. If you've owned a hunting dog, you can sympathize. This dog never sits still. And if she doesn't get exercise, she'll bounce off the walls for days. The best exercise Heidi gets is when she's out chasing squirrels. She runs like hell after those furry little rodents, but she's yet to make a kill. That's because squirrels are elusive little varmints who have a great instinct for self-survival.

Trying to bag a Squirrel in golf may be equally as hard. The object of the game is to win four holes while playing with a four-some. (You could play Squirrel against one opponent or two, but the game's challenge is enhanced with four players.) Before heading out for your round, set up a pot with everybody throwing in the same amount of money. Tied holes don't win nor are they carried over to the next hole. A hole has to be won outright. The first player to win four holes wins the pot. If a player wins four holes before the end of the round, and there are enough holes remaining to start another game, you may want to go at it again.

Hawk is one of my favorite games; it's best played with four players, but can be played with three. Before starting your round, one person is picked as the Hawk.

After everybody tees off, the Hawk now must choose a partner to play against the two other players. The team with the best ball wins the hole. Ties are thrown out. On ensuing holes, a new Hawk is selected and the process begins anew. Things can get interesting if the Hawk elects the option of not selecting a partner. In this case, the hole's value is doubled and if the Hawk loses, he pays everyone double the value of the hole. By the 17th and 18th holes, each player should have been the Hawk four times. The player who's losing the most bets then becomes the Hawk for the last two holes. When playing Hawk in a threesome, a bogey score is posted for a "phantom" fourth player. Play is the same as foursome Hawk.

Best Ball
Odd and
Even

Remember those crazy rules during the '70s gas crisis? If you had a car with an odd-numbered license plate, you could only get gasoline on certain days of the week; if you had an even-numbered plate, you had to fill up on the alternate days. And I don't even remember what the rule was for vanity plates. Seems to me I remember some enterprising, hot-blooded teenagers easily getting around the system. Especially if they had a date 40 miles away and date night fell on their "off" day. All they had to do was change the plates on their cars. Don't look at me. My girlfriends lived within walking distance. But I do know several romantics who risked big fines–all for the sake of a long distance tryst.

In Best Ball Odd and Even, your fine is heavily weighted on how you and your partner play. Played as a foursome, each player drives alternately on odd- or even- numbered holes. The partner of the player who didn't drive the hole then follows up with the second shot. Team players then alternate hitting the ball, on the fairway and green, until it's dropped in. The team that holes out with the lowest score wins the hole.

This game is one of the formats played by the pros during the Ryder Cup. Some folks think that the pressure of this game is on the player who's driving the hole. Others say that fairway and green play is the major factor. All players being equal, it probably makes no difference at all. Regardless of how it's tilted, if at all, it's a game that's best played (and watched) when low handicap players make up the foursome. Quickly now, is your license plate odd or even?

Arnies
and
Jacks

Comedy had Laurel and Hardy. Yankee fans will always remember Mantle and Maris. The rock and roll crowd admired Simon and Garfunkel. All these names are indelibly etched into our consciousness as great icons in Americana. But certainly nobody could mistake the names of Palmer and Nicklaus as a slapstick comedy team, a pair of home run hitters or two kids from New York crooning about teenage rites of passage. Palmer and Nicklaus will always be legendary names among the dimpled ball crowd.

Arnie's Army was one of the most popular and spirited gang of spectators this side of the Chicago Cubs' bleacher bums. They religiously followed their amiable leader up and down the fairways, and sometimes off them, too. It is for this reason we have a bet in his honor. Arnies is a bet where a player wins a hole and has made par after never being on the fairway. We've all been there at one time or another, and in a perverse sort of way, making par after you've been spraying the ball all over the place can add real excitement to your game. To use a baseball term, it's winning ugly. Throw in an Arnie as a side bet and you'll be in seventh heaven.

Jacks, on the hand, is for the long hitter crowd. It's a side bet that rewards the player for the longest drive on a hole. The good thing is if you try too hard to win a Jack and you drive your ball onto an adjacent fairway, you're now eligible to win an Arnie. Either way you're in good company.

Jacks, like Arnies, can be in play on all holes, or you can choose certain holes either by nines or total round. When playing Arnies and Jacks, par 3s are usually thrown out.

Hogans
and
Lone
Ranger

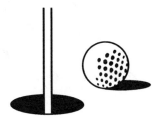

I'm convinced that much of the slow play on the golf course is caused by Walter Mitty types who fancy themselves as professional golfers. They love to emulate what they think is the pros' pre-stroke technique. They spend an endless amount of time dawdling over the ball, studying the breaks of the greens, or figuring out what the sea level, wind resistance, and barometric pressure are on a tee box. Unfortunately, their game usually doesn't measure up to their dallying behavior. They are the most chronic slicers, shankers and duffers in the group. By the time the dust clears, they haven't broken 100 and you're working on a five hours plus round. Rounds like that are excruciating and if I know a guy dawdles, I stay away from him like the plague.

Betting a Hogan is the antithesis of marathon golf and is what the professional game is all about. An economical round of golf. Named after golf great Ben Hogan, Hogan is a bet that rewards exacting play and works this way. Any golfer who lands on the fairway, hits the green in regulation and then goes on to make par or better on the hole wins a Hogan. Case closed. It's a game that's geared for the better player and can be in play throughout the whole round or on declared holes. It's a good bet that if you're playing with a group who's pocketing Hogans, you'll be at the 19th hole in regulation time.

Lone Ranger is a fun game that's best played with three players, although it certainly can be played with four. One golfer plays the hole against the other two players, and his score is matched against the worst ball of his opponents. So if I'm playing Steve and Ed and I shoot a bogey 5, Steve shoots a bogey 5 but Ed shoots the worst ball, a double bogey 6, I win the hole. To structure the game for three players, you can divide the 18 holes in sequential groups of six, or randomly assign holes. With four players, play 16 holes and throw out two par 3 holes.

Two or Foursome Scotch

Here's some revisionist golf history that's bound to get me run out of Edinburgh and banned from the St. Andrews Golf Club. Contrary to popular belief, our most beloved game was invented by the Dutch, and not by the Scots. It's said that the game actually started out in Holland and was known as "colf." Some golf historians have advanced the theory that the game then made its way to Scotland when it jumped over the North Sea. The Scots, knowing a good game when they play it, immediately claimed it as their own. Scottish shepherds were the first to pick up the game when they passed time hitting stones in rabbit holes with their crooks. Makes sense to me. Can't think of a better way to kill time when you're tending sheep all day.

Notwithstanding this historical and quite possibly hysterical hypothesis, let's talk about a game called Scotch. Although it can be played with any number of players, the best fun is with four golfers. Let's say I'm playing with three of my buddies, with Steve as my partner, playing against Ed and Nick. We decide on a playing order in which I tee off first to start the round. Steve (my partner) must hit my second shot, while Ed's partner, Nick, hits their second shot. We keep this pattern of play throughout the whole round. In other words, we alternate shots. Play continues this way until the ball is holed out. As opposed to some other alternately played games, there's no set "driver" in this game. The player who holes out the previous hole defers to his partner to drive the next hole.

If you're playing match play, and you hit when you're not supposed to, you automatically lose the hole. If you're playing stroke play, then an incorrect shooting order results in two penalty strokes. If you're playing as a threesome, then one player plays his ball, while the other two play one ball.

Replay
or
Do Over

Besides being the name of a great-tasting fish, fluke is a derisive term that applies to unbelievable shots on the golf course. Most of the time the term is whispered under our breath especially after an opponent has made the shot of his life. Usually, we camouflage our true feelings by congratulating our opponent with an "Atta Boy!" or an enthusiastic high five, all the while muttering to ourselves what a fluke shot it was. I've never liked this type of phoniness, especially when I'm playing with friends. That's why I enjoy Replay or Do Over, a game that takes away all that fake sportsmanship. If you decide to play this game, though, I recommend that you do so with close friends. Very close friends.

Replay can be played with two,

three or four players. If you're playing with four players, you then play teams. The premise of the game is that you have the right to have your opponent(s) replay four shots throughout the round. And, in turn, they have the same right against you and your partner. So if you've crushed a great drive, tagged a tremendous fairway shot over a lake hazard or drained a 60-foot putt, your opponents can ask you to replay the shot. And regardless of how your shot lands, better, worse or the same, it's the second shot that counts.

So if your playing buddy hits the shot of his life, and you ask him to shoot again, beware. He may not have the same perspective on the game as you originally thought. He may gnash his teeth and call you all kinds of names. Then again, he may smile. He'll probably call you all kinds of names later. Replay can be played in either match or stroke format.

Bucket
of
Points

When I was growing up in New York City, we played a lively street game called points. Points was a game that was played with a rubber ball (called a Spaldeen in New York City lingo), thrown against a stoop. For those of you not familiar with the term "stoop", it's the name for the steps leading up to a residential building, like the steps going up into a Victorian house or brownstone. We'd spend hours playing points. You'd throw the ball against the stoop, and collect points if it hit the "point" of the stair. You held your turn until you dropped the ball. It was a great game to pass the time and provides terrific memories for ex-street kids who will, given the chance, wax nostalgic about their exploits. I once interviewed the NBC sportscaster Marv Albert. Marv grew up in Brooklyn and one of his passions was playing points. He loved the game so much that he still plays today. For one of his milestone birthdays, his wife had a stoop built behind his house.

Bucket of Points is another type of game you could easily fall in love with. It can be played with any number of players. Essentially, you collect points on the golf course by using the following scoring system:

> Eagle.................6 points
> Birdie ....5 points
> Par.....................4 points
> Bogey................2 points

The trick to collecting points on the golf course is the same as collecting stoopball points. Don't pay any attention to what the other golfers are doing, just go about your business and collect the most points you can. The player who collects the most points after 18 holes is the winner. Payouts are determined by computing the point differences among the players.

Vegas
Shootout

"THIS TURKEY IS GOING TO BE EASY"

WARDELL 93

I had a poker friend named Sal who turned into a nervous wreck every time he sat at a high stakes table in Las Vegas. In addition to breaking out in a cold sweat, he would always find a way to embarrass himself. It was a shame because he was decent card player, but put him in a game with high stakes and he'd develop the mental yips. The worst incident was the time we were playing at Caesar's Palace, right after he took a hit on twenty-one. When the exasperated dealer told him he had unnecessarily busted out, Sal dropped his cigarette on the card table. Nervously trying to swipe the burning ashes off the felt, he knocked over his gin and tonic. Ice cubes and Tanqueray were everywhere. He politely excused himself and walked out of the casino.

If you're like my nervous-nellie friend and have a tendency to fold up like a cheap suit when the stakes get high, then you may want to think again before playing Vegas Shootout. This game is played as a foursome, with scores of the team players bundled as one. Here's an example. Steve is my partner and we're playing against Ed and Nick. Steve and I shoot two par 4s. Ed shoots a bogey 5 and Nick shoots a double bogey 6. For the hole Steve and I have shot a 44, while Ed and Nick have shot a 56. The lower number of the score is usually, but not always, placed first. The difference in our scores is 12 points. If we were playing $5 per point, Steve and I win $60 for the hole. Things get interesting when birdies or eagles come into play. If a team member shoots a birdie, the point difference is doubled. If a team member shoots an eagle, the point difference is tripled.

Here's another variation: If a winning team player shoots a birdie or eagle, the losing team is required to reverse their score by placing the higher score first. Example: I shoot a birdie 3 and my partner Steve shoots a par 4. Ed shoots a double bogey 6 and Nick shoots a bogey 5. Under the rules of regular Vegas Shootout, the point difference is 22 points (56-34=22 points). But if you're playing reverse, the point difference is 31 points (65-34=31 points). What bet gets doubled and what doesn't is up to you and your group, and should be decided upon beforehand. Whichever way you play it, Vegas Shootout can cost lots of money and isn't for the faint of heart.

Putting
Bets

There are probably more betting games designed for putting than for any other part of the game. We all know knocking it in the hole when you're on the carpet is the most critical part of the game. Here are a few betting games that will help you sharpen your putting skills.

Tally Putts

The name says it all. During a round every player keeps score of his putting strokes. The player with the fewest putts after the round wins the Tally Putts bet. Several variations: Any player who three putts two holes must add a +2 to his overall putting score. A player who three putts three holes, add +3 to his overall putting score.

Three Putt Dare

Let's say you're playing with a guy who you know is a lousy putter. He's sixty feet and three breaks away from the hole. In this game, you challenge him to a bet that he will three putt the hole. He accepts. If he one putts the hole, he wins the bet, triple the amount. If he two putts, the bet is a push. If he three putts, you win the bet.

Best Putts

Play all 9 or 18 holes on the practice green. The winner of the previous hole elects which hole to shoot for next. The player with the fewest number of strokes wins.

Blocking Putts

This is another practice green game with two players shooting two balls apiece. Blocking the hole with your ball is perfectly legitimate.

The game is scored on a point system:

-first player 1 putts, he gets 3 points;

-second player 1 putts, he gets 6 points;

-closest to the hole, 1 point;

-two balls from the same player closest to he hole, score 2 points.

-two consecutive 1 putts, score 6 points.

-first player 1 putts both balls, score 5 points

-second player 1 putts both balls, (if first player hasn't), 12 points.

Play is around the 18 practice green holes. The winner is the player with the highest number of points after play. Played holes are decided upon by the previous hole winner. However, no two holes can be played twice.

Criers'
Tourney

"CRYBABY WARD. QUIET PLEASE."

I've saved this bet for last. And for good reason. It's a 19th hole game played when everybody's crying in their beer.

Golf brings out the crybaby in all of us. We will whine, gripe, moan, sigh, snivel and whimper about the smallest little misfortune that happens to prey upon us during a round of golf. Some of the whining is warranted. Most of it isn't. And the 19th hole is the place where we crybabies hold court. We make excuses ranging from the distracting decibel level of the bird crowing in a tree to the arthritic metacarpal in our index finger. We bellyache about how we could have broken 90 if we had worn our lucky sweater. Or curse the low-lying branch that snagged a great punch shot. No wonder our loved ones pass us a mop to wipe up our tears and then turn a deaf ear. They've been down this road many, many times before.

Criers' Tourney is for the crybaby who takes his whining to another level. The golfer who swears that if he didn't have to play that par 5, 505-yard dogleg, he'd beat you every time. Or if that par 3 125-yard hole, which demands a wedge shot (his worst club), wasn't on the course, he'd pick your pocket clean. Or how he really believes he is a better golfer than you, if only the course was 16 holes. Most of us can handle garden variety whining. But where whining ends and obnoxious behavior begins is when a golfer really thinks one hole is going to make a difference in his otherwise lousy game.

Criers' Tourney can be played with any number of players and is a stroke play bet. After the round, each player chooses two or three of his worst holes and changes them back to par. After the holes have been selected and the holes rescored, strokes are counted and bets are paid based on the player who has the lowest score. For those super crybabies who feel that one or two holes will make a radical difference, the results can be startling and eye-opening.

The 19th Hole

THANKS for buying our book! Send us your name and we'll send you a free gift! And if you have any good bets or golf stories to tell, we'd like to hear about them.

Write to: GolfBooks
            P.O. Box 43238
            Upper Montclair, NJ 07043

Order a copy of <u>Bet On Your Golf Game!</u> for a friend.

Name _____

Address _____

City _____ State ___ Zip _____

Make your check payable to GolfBooks. Send $7.95 plus $3.00 for shipping and handling to GolfBooks, P.O. Box 43238, Upper Montclair, New Jersey 07043.
Credit Card Orders: 1-800-723-4620
Sales Tax: New Jersey residents must add 6% sales tax with order.

Please allow three to four weeks delivery.